THE
TOTALLY
MUFFINS
COOKBOOK

Printed in Singapore.

The Totally Muffins cookbook is produced by becker&mayer!, Ltd.

Cover illustration and design: Dick Witt

Interior design and typesetting: Susan Hernday

Interior illustrations: Carolyn Vibbert

Library of Congress Cataloging-in-Publication Data
Siegel, Helene.
    Totally Muffins Cookbook / by Helene Siegel and Karen Gillingham.
       p.   cm.
    ISBN 0-89087-756-4
    1. Muffins   I. Gillingham, Karen.   II. Title.
TX770. M83S53   1995
641.8'15—dc20

95-13579
CIP

Celestial Arts Publishing
P.O. Box 7123
Berkeley, CA 94707

Other cookbooks in this series:
The Totally Garlic Cookbook
The Totally Chile Pepper Cookbook
The Totally Mushroom Cookbook
The Totally Corn Cookbook
The Totally Cookies Cookbook
The Totally Teatime Cookbook
The Totally Coffee Cookbook

THE
TOTALLY
MUFFINS
COOKBOOK

by
Helene Siegel
and
Karen Gillingham

Illustrations by Carolyn Vibbert

CELESTIAL ARTS
BERKELEY, CA

Do you know the muffin man,
The muffin man, the muffin man?
Do you know the muffin man?
He lives in Drury Lane.

If you are a muffin eater or even a muffin nibbler, you owe it to yourself to become a muffin baker. No other form of baking offers such high return for such low investment.

All it takes is about ten minutes mixing time and twenty minutes baking time to whip out the freshest, tangiest blueberry muffins, the most wholesome nutty brown cranberry muffins, carrot muffins that beg to be eaten, and dark chocolate cherry muffins rich enough to pass for dessert.

It doesn't take any fancy equipment or culinary technique to achieve results that almost always surpass the lead-weight, chemically enhanced store-bought kind.

Muffins, the handheld answer to cake, are an American phenomenon of the last 150 years. They owe their existence to the development of chemical leaveners like baking soda and powder that speed up

the rising process.
Our collection of simple, honest,
all-American goodies is arranged in four
categories for easy access: classic muffins for
purists who crave nothing more than a perfect
blueberry or banana nut muffin to start their day;
party muffins for sweet tooths who crave illicit thrills
like chewy caramel apple muffins or vanilla-spiked
macadamia cake with their afternoon coffee; savory
muffins with flavorings like aniseed, caraway, potatoes,
fresh herbs, and chile peppers to provide a tasty bread
or roll alternative for quick suppers; and health
muffins for those who are always on the lookout for
healthful but delicious snacks. Be warned, however,
our definition of "good for you" is a loose one.
These muffins are packed with bran, oats, nuts,
seeds, vegetables, and herbs but they also have
things like sugar and buttermilk to balance and
enhance the flavors. So all you need to do is
follow the recipes and excellent muffins are
sure to follow. Remember—if everyone loves
a good muffin, the muffin maker must be a
pretty popular person.

Baking Soda vs. Powder

Baking soda and baking powder give muffins the boost they need to rise in minutes, rather than the hours it takes a yeast dough to rise. Here is how the two differ:

Baking soda, or sodium bicarbonate, is always used in combination with a sour ingredient like sour cream, buttermilk, yogurt or lemon juice. The general rule is ½ teaspoon soda for each cup sour liquid or tablespoon lemon juice. Baking soda is activated as soon as it gets wet, so bake quickly when it is used alone.

Baking powder, a combination of baking soda, two acids and cornstarch, is easier to work with. Since the acid is already added it does not need anything to neutralize it and since it is double acting you have a little more time to get things in the oven. It starts bubbling first when liquid is applied and again with heat. The hotter the oven, the better and quicker the rise.

When in doubt, rely on baking powder. The general rule is 1½ teaspoons powder to each cup flour. Each ½ teaspoon soda replaces 2 teaspoons powder. For all-purpose muffin baking, you can't go wrong with 1 tablespoon baking powder.

CONVERSIONS

Liquid

1 Tbsp = 15 ml

1/2 cup = 2 fl. oz = 60 ml

1 cup = 8 fl. oz = 250 ml

Dry

1/4 cup = 4 Tbsp = 2 oz = 60 g

1 cup = 1/2 pound = 8 oz = 250 g

Flour

1/2 cup = 60 g

1 cup = 4 oz = 125 g

Temperature

400° F = 200°C = gas mark 6

375° F = 190°C = gas mark 5

350°F = 175°C = gas mark 4

Miscellaneous

2 Tbsp butter = 1 oz = 30 g

1 inch = 2.5 cm

all-purpose flour = plain flour

baking soda = bicarbonate of soda

brown sugar = demerara sugar

confectioners' sugar = icing sugar

heavy cream = double cream

molasses = black treacle

raisins = sultanas

rolled oats = oat flakes

semisweet chocolate = plain chocolate

sugar = caster sugar

Classic
Muffins

BLUEBERRY BUTTERMILK MUFFINS

In a world of earthquakes and blizzards, isn't it reassuring to know that great blueberry muffins need only be minutes away? For best results, do not defrost frozen berries.

6 tablespoons butter, softened
²/₃ cup sugar
2 eggs
1 cup buttermilk
2 teaspoons vanilla
2¼ cups all-purpose flour
½ teaspoon salt
1 teaspoon baking soda
2 teaspoons baking powder
½ teaspoon nutmeg
1½ cups blueberries,
   fresh or frozen (unthawed)

Preheat oven to 400 degrees F. Grease muffin tins or line with paper cups.

Cream butter and sugar until light and fluffy. Add eggs, buttermilk, and vanilla. Lightly beat until blended.

In another bowl, stir together flour, salt, baking soda, powder, and nutmeg. Add dry mixture to liquid and stir just until flour disappears.

Gently stir berries into batter and fill muffin cups to top. Bake 20 minutes. Let cool 5 minutes. Turn out and cool before serving.

MAKES 12

BANANA WALNUT MUFFINS

The basic banana muffin—one of the best reasons we know for getting up in the morning.

¾ cup chopped walnuts
2 cups all-purpose flour
1 tablespoon baking powder
½ teaspoon salt
1 stick butter, softened
¾ cup brown sugar
2 eggs
1½ teaspoons vanilla
1½ cups mashed ripe bananas (about 3)

Preheat oven to 375 degrees F. Grease muffin tins or line with paper cups.

Spread nuts on a tray and toast in oven 8 to 10 minutes. Set aside.

In a bowl, combine flour, baking powder and salt.

In another bowl, cream butter, sugar, and vanilla until smooth and creamy. Beat in eggs one at a time. Add mashed bananas and beat until combined.

Stir dry ingredients into banana mixture just until flour disappears. Lightly stir in nuts.

Spoon batter into muffin cups to the top. Bake 20 to 25 minutes, until toothpick comes out clean.

MAKES 12

On Mixing

Muffins need very little stirring to achieve the proper consistency. Three or four strokes with a big wooden spoon for the final combining is generally enough. If you can no longer see streaks of white flour, it is time to stop, even if the batter looks lumpy. The aim of muffin mixing is not to beat in air, as it is with cake mixing. Over mixing leads to tough muffins.

PUMPKIN CURRANT MUFFINS

These wholesome pumpkin-packed muffins feel so much more virtuous than pie for breakfast. They are great with some thin slices of good cheddar cheese.

1 1/2 cups all-purpose flour
2 teaspoons baking powder
1/4 teaspoon salt
1/2 teaspoon cinnamon
1/4 teaspoon ground ginger
pinch nutmeg
2 eggs
1/4 cup molasses
1/3 cup brown sugar
1/4 cup vegetable oil
1 cup canned pumpkin puree
1/2 cup currants

Preheat oven to 400 degrees F. Grease muffin tins or line with paper cups.

In a large bowl combine flour, baking powder, salt, cinnamon, ginger, and nutmeg.

In another bowl, whisk together eggs, brown sugar, molasses, oil, and pumpkin. Add to flour mixture and mix with spoon until flour just disappears. Stir in currants.

Spoon into muffin cups and bake 20 to 25 minutes, until tester comes out clean.

MAKES 10 TO 12

Quickbreads

Muffin recipes can be converted to quick-breads by baking in a greased loaf pan at 350 degrees F. for about an hour.

APPLESAUCE SPICE MUFFINS

These cinnamony brown apple muffins are moist on the inside and crisp on top.

1¾ cups all-purpose flour
2½ teaspoons baking powder
1½ teaspoons cinnamon
½ teaspoon salt
¼ teaspoon ground cloves
2 eggs
½ cup + 2 tablespoons brown sugar
¼ cup vegetable oil
½ cup milk
1 cup diced peeled apple such as Fuji
   or Golden Delicious
1 tablespoon lemon juice
½ cup applesauce
½ teaspoon cinnamon mixed with 3
   tablespoons sugar for topping

Preheat oven
to 375 degrees F.
Grease or line muffin
tins with paper cups.

Combine flour, baking powder, cinnamon, salt,
and cloves in medium bowl.

In another large bowl, whisk together eggs,
sugar, oil, milk, apple, lemon juice, and applesauce. Add flour mixture to liquid ingredients
and stir just until flour disappears.

Spoon into muffin cups. Spinkle tops with
cinnamon sugar mixture and bake 25 to 30
minutes until tester comes out clean.

MAKES 12

STRAWBERRY STREUSEL MUFFINS

Streusel topping approaches perfection atop this muffin.

STREUSEL TOPPING:

½ stick butter
½ cup brown sugar
½ teaspoon cinnamon
pinch of salt
⅔ cup all-purpose flour

MUFFINS

1 stick butter, softened
⅔ cup sugar
2 eggs
1 teaspoon vanilla
¾ cup milk
1¾ cups all-purpose flour
2½ teaspoons baking powder
¼ teaspoon salt
1½ cups firm, ripe strawberries, hulled
and roughly chopped

To make streusel: Cream together butter and brown sugar until smooth. Add cinnamon and salt; mix until blended. Add flour and mix with fingertips or pastry blender just until crumbly. Streusel can be made in advance and refrigerated up to a week.

Preheat oven to 375 degrees F. Grease or line muffin tins with paper cups.

Cream together butter and sugar until light and smooth. Add eggs, vanilla, and milk. Lightly beat until smooth.

In another bowl, combine flour, baking powder and salt. Add to liquid ingredients and stir just until flour disappears. Gently stir in berries. Spoon into muffin cups and sprinkle tops with streusel. Bake about 25 minutes, or until a tester comes out clean.

MAKES 12

BASIC CORN MUFFINS

A basic light, bright yellow corn muffin, with a slight tang from buttermilk. Delicious served warm with honey.

¾ cup all-purpose flour
¾ cup yellow cornmeal
2 teaspoons baking powder
1 teaspoon baking soda
1 tablespoon sugar
½ teaspoon salt
1 egg
1 cup buttermilk
½ stick butter, melted and cooled

Preheat oven to 400 degrees F. Grease muffin tins or line with paper cups.

Combine flour, cornmeal, baking powder, baking soda, salt, and sugar in a bowl. Mix with a fork.

In another bowl, whisk egg until smooth. Whisk in buttermilk and melted butter to combine. Pour into flour mixture and stir until evenly moistened. Fill muffin cups three-quarters full and bake 15 to 20 minutes, or until a tester comes out clean.

MAKES 9

Filling the Cups

For full, beautifully rounded muffin tops, fill cups all the way to the top.

As for paper liners, we thoroughly endorse them. With paper cups, muffins are guaranteed to come out of the pan first time, every time. They make washing the pan a breeze; eliminate the need to grease and keep muffins fresh longer.

If your muffins are sticking to the papers, you are probably trying to eat them too soon. Once thoroughly cooled, papers should peel easily.

REFRIGERATOR BRAN MUFFINS

In addition to its fine taste this bran muffin is extremely convenient. The batter can be refrigerated for up to 4 weeks and baked as needed—handy for impromptu weekend brunches or large families. The recipe is from Michele Fuetsch of Los Angeles and Cleveland.

2 cups bran cereal
1 cup boiling water
2½ cups whole wheat flour
2½ teaspoons baking soda
½ teaspoon salt
2 eggs
1 cup sugar
2 cups buttermilk
1 stick butter, melted
¼ cup wheat germ

Preheat oven to 375 degrees F. Grease or line muffin tins with paper cups. In large mixing bowl, combine bran with boiling water. Stir and set aside to soften.

In medium bowl, combine whole wheat flour, baking soda, and salt. Set aside.

In another bowl, whisk eggs until smooth. Whisk in sugar. Add remaining ingredients and gently whisk. (Do not be concerned with curdling.) Pour buttermilk mixture into bran and stir well. Stir in flour mixture.

Fill muffin cups and bake 20 to 25 minutes, until a tester comes out clean. Store batter in a covered container in the refrigerator for up to four weeks.

MAKES 18

CARROT RAISIN MUFFINS

*These moist, spicy muffins will dispel any overly sweet,
leaden carrot experiences from your memory bank.*

2 eggs
$\frac{1}{2}$ cup + 2 tablespoons vegetable oil
$\frac{1}{2}$ cup sugar
1 $\frac{1}{2}$ cups coarsely grated carrot
$\frac{1}{2}$ cup raisins
$\frac{3}{4}$ cup walnuts, toasted and chopped
1 $\frac{1}{2}$ cups all-purpose flour
2 $\frac{1}{4}$ teaspoons baking powder
$\frac{1}{4}$ teaspoon salt
1 $\frac{1}{2}$ teaspoons cinnamon
$\frac{1}{2}$ teaspon nutmeg

Preheat oven to 400 degrees F. Grease or line muffin tins with paper cups.

In large mixing bowl, whisk eggs, oil and sugar until smooth. Stir in carrots, raisins, and $\frac{1}{2}$ cup of nuts.

In another bowl, stir together remaining ingredients except nuts. Add flour mixture to carrot mixture and stir well to combine. (This is a stiff batter.)

Spoon into muffin cups and sprinkle tops with remaining nuts. Bake about 25 minutes, until a tester comes out clean.

MAKES 10

ALMOND POPPY SEED MUFFINS

We love the double crunch of poppy seeds and nuts in these classic morning muffins.

²/₃ cup milk
½ cup poppy seeds
1 ½ cups all-purpose flour
2 teaspoons baking powder
½ teaspoon baking soda
¼ teaspoon salt
1 stick butter, softened
¾ cup sugar
2 eggs
½ teaspoon almond extract
½ cup sliced almonds

Preheat oven to 350 degrees F. Grease muffin tins or line with paper cups.

Heat milk to scalding. Pour over poppy seeds and set aside to cool.

In a bowl, combine flour, baking powder, baking soda, and salt.

In another large bowl, cream butter and sugar until light. Beat in eggs, one at a time, beating well after each addition. Stir in almond extract and cooled milk mixture.

Fold in dry ingredients and almonds and stir just to blend.

Divide mixture among muffin cups. Bake about 20 minutes or until tester comes out clean.

MAKES 12

APRICOT SOURDOUGH MUFFINS

The easiest way to make a sourough starter is from a commercial mix. Most mixes require several days to cultivate, so plan ahead. Starter can be kept indefinitely in the refrigerator.

$\frac{1}{2}$ cup sourdough starter,
    room temperature
$\frac{1}{2}$ cup plain low fat yogurt
2 cups all-purpose flour
$\frac{1}{2}$ cup sugar
1 stick butter, melted
1 egg, lightly beaten
1 teaspoon baking soda
1 teaspoon baking powder
$\frac{1}{2}$ teaspoon salt
$\frac{1}{2}$ teaspoon cinnamon
1 cup chopped dried apricots
$\frac{1}{2}$ cup chopped hazelnuts

Preheat oven to 375 degrees F. Grease muffin tins or line with paper cups.

In large bowl, combine starter, yogurt and ½ cup flour.

Stir in sugar, melted butter, and egg just to blend.

Combine remaining flour with baking soda, baking powder, salt and cinnamon. Stir into starter mixture just until moistened. Gently stir in apricots and hazelnuts. Spoon into prepared muffin cups. Bake 25 minutes, until tester comes out clean.

MAKES 12

DATE NUT MUFFINS

One of our favorite vehicles for cream cheese.

2 cups all-purpose flour
½ cup sugar
1 teaspoon baking powder
1 teaspoon baking soda
1 teaspoon cinnamon
¼ teaspoon salt
1 (8 ounce) package chopped,
    pitted dates
¾ cup chopped pecans
3 tablespoons butter
1 teaspoon vanilla
1 cup hot milk
1 egg, lightly beaten

Preheat oven to 400 degrees F. Grease muffin tins or line with paper cups.

In bowl, combine flour, sugar, baking powder, soda, cinnamon, and salt. Stir in dates and nuts.

In another bowl, stir butter and vanilla with hot milk until butter melts. Blend in egg. Add to dry ingredients and stir just until blended.

Spoon into muffin cups. Bake 20 minutes or until tester comes out clean.

MAKES 12

Advance Preparations

A quick tip for those who crave hot morning muffins but don't have much time in the morning. Dry and liquid ingredients can be mixed up to a day in advance and stored separately. Refrigerate the liquid if it will be sitting for more than a couple of hours. Combine liquid and dry mixtures when the oven is hot and ready to bake.

BUTTER-DIPPED PEAR MUFFINS

These tender, sweet muffins are special enough to serve with your best afternoon tea.

2 cups peeled and chopped fresh pears
1 cup sugar
1 stick butter, melted and cooled
2 eggs, lightly beaten
1 teaspoon vanilla
1 ½ cups all-purpose flour
1 teaspoon baking powder
1 teaspoon baking soda
½ teaspoon salt
½ cup coarsely chopped walnuts
1 teaspoon cinnamon
½ teaspoon ground nutmeg
½ teaspoon ground allspice
3 tablespoons hot melted butter

Preheat oven to 350 degrees F. Grease muffin tins or line with paper cups.

In large bowl, toss pears with ¾ cup sugar. Set aside.

In separate bowl, blend cooled melted butter, eggs, and vanilla.

In third bowl, combine flour, baking powder, soda and salt. Stir in nuts.

Stir egg mixture into pears. Sprinkle flour mixture over pear mixture and stir to blend. Spoon into prepared muffin cups and bake 20 minutes or until tester comes out clean.

Turn out onto rack.

In small shallow bowl, mix cinnamon, nutmeg and allspice with remaining ¼ cup sugar. When cool enough to handle, dip each muffin top first in hot melted butter then in spice mixture. Serve warm.

MAKES 9

HEALTH MUFFINS

WHOLE WHEAT CRANBERRY MUFFINS

We love the intense burst of flavor that comes from keeping the berries whole in these wheat bran muffins.

1 cup all-bran cereal
1 1/4 cups milk
1 egg, beaten
1/4 cup vegetable oil
1 tablespoon grated orange zest
1 1/2 cups whole wheat flour
1/2 cup sugar
1 tablespoon baking powder
1/4 teaspoon salt
1 cup cranberries, fresh or frozen
  (unthawed)
3/4 cup walnuts, toasted and chopped

Preheat oven to 400 degrees F. Grease or line muffin tins with paper cups.

Combine bran and milk in a bowl and set aside to soften for 5 minutes.

In another large bowl, mix together whole wheat flour, sugar, baking powder, and salt with a fork.

Add egg, oil, and zest to bran mixture. Stir to combine. Pour into dry ingredients and stir until evenly moistened. Stir in nuts and cranberries. Spoon into muffin cups. Bake about 20 minutes, until tester comes out clean.

MAKES 12

MAPLE OATMEAL MUFFINS

Our favorite oatmeal toppings are mixed into a nubbly brown muffin.

> 2 eggs
> ½ cup brown sugar
> 1 1/4 cups buttermilk
> ¾ cup maple syrup
> 1¼ cups whole wheat flour
> 1½ cups rolled oats + 3 tablespoons for sprinkling
> 1 teaspoon baking powder
> 1 teaspoon baking soda
> ½ teaspoon salt

Preheat oven to 400 degrees F. Grease muffin tins or line with paper cups.

Whisk together eggs and brown sugar until smooth. Add buttermilk and maple syrup. Whisk and set aside.

In another bowl, combine wheat flour, 1½ cups of oats, baking powder, soda, and salt. Mix with fork. Add to buttermilk mixture and stir until evenly moistened. Spoon into muffin cups, to the top. Spinkle about a teaspoon rolled oats across the top and bake 20 minutes, until a tester comes out clean.

MAKES 12

GRANOLA MUFFINS

1 stick butter, melted
¾ cup sugar
2 eggs, lightly beaten
½ cup milk
1½ cups all-purpose flour
1 tablespoon baking powder
½ teaspoon salt
1½ cups unsweetened granola
½ cup dried cherries, blueberries,
   cranberries, strawberries or mixture

Preheat oven to 350 degrees F. Grease muffin tins or line with paper cups.

In large bowl, blend butter, sugar, eggs, and milk.

In another bowl, mix flour with baking powder and salt.

Gradually add to liquid ingredients, stirring just to blend.

Stir in granola and dried fruit. Divide batter equally among muffin cups. Bake 25 to 30 minutes or until muffins spring back when lightly pressed.

MAKES 10

The Butter Thing

Butter is our first choice for the more delicately flavored cakelike muffins. We always use unsalted for its freshness, and add a bit of salt to the batter for flavor. These tasty muffins will not need to be slathered with anything when they are done— they will be moist and flavorful.

DOUBLE BRAN MUFFINS

Get a double dose of bran in these wholesome treats.

1 cup bran cereal
1 cup oat bran
1¼ cups all-purpose flour
2 teaspoons baking soda
½ teaspoon salt
2 eggs
1 cup buttermilk
⅓ cup honey
½ cup vegetable oil
¾ cup chopped prunes (optional)

Preheat oven to 400 degrees F. Grease muffin tins or line with paper cups.

In bowl, combine brans, flour, baking soda, and salt.

In another bowl, beat eggs. Beat in buttermilk, honey, and oil. Add to dry ingredients and stir just to blend. Fold in prunes, if desired. Divide batter among muffin cups and bake about 20 minutes or until tops spring back when lightly pressed.

MAKES 12

Fruity Muffins

Fruits add flavor, sweetness and moisture to muffins. Since delicate flavors are easily overwhelmed by baking, dried fruits are a great alternative to fresh. In addition to traditional raisins and currants, dried cranberries, blueberries, and sour cherries are now widely available. Any of these bite-sized fruits can be used interchangeably and all can be plumped, in hot water if too dry, or for more flavor, use a liqueur or fruit juice.

SUNFLOWER WHEAT MUFFINS

These virtuous muffins are packed with a cupful of luscious sunflower seeds.

1 cup shelled, unsalted sunflower seeds
1 cup all-purpose flour
1 cup whole wheat flour
1 tablespoon baking powder
$\frac{1}{2}$ teaspoon salt
1 egg
$\frac{1}{4}$ cup vegetable oil
3 tablespoons honey
1 cup low-fat milk

Preheat oven to 375 degrees F. Grease muffin tins or line with paper cups.

Place ⅓ cup sunflower seeds in blender or food processor. Process until finely ground.

In large bowl, combine ground seeds, flours, baking powder, and salt.

In small bowl, beat egg. Stir in oil, honey, and milk.

Add to dry ingredients and stir just to blend. Stir in remaining sunflower seeds. Divide among muffin cups.

Bake about 25 minutes or until tops spring back when lightly touched.

MAKES 9

PUMPKIN SEED SQUASH MUFFINS

These brightly colored muffins would be a nice accompaniment to a spicy stew.

2 cups all-purpose flour
2 tablespoons sugar
1½ teaspoons baking powder
1½ teaspoons dried thyme or sage, crumbled
½ teaspoon ground nutmeg
½ teaspoon salt
1 (12-ounce) package frozen, pureed cooked squash, thawed (1cup)
1 stick butter, melted
2 eggs
1 cup shelled, unsalted pumpkin seeds

Preheat oven to 400 degrees F. Grease muffin tins or line with paper cups.

In large bowl, combine flour, sugar, baking powder, thyme or sage, nutmeg, and salt.

In another bowl, mix squash with butter and eggs.

Pour into dry ingredients and stir just until blended. Stir in pumpkin seeds. Divide batter among muffin cups.

Bake 20 minutes or until tops spring back when lightly touched.

MAKES 12

Storing Muffins

We like to pack leftover muffins in ziplock bags and store in the freezer, where they will keep as long as three months. Defrost in a 350 degree F. oven about 10 minutes. Toaster ovens are perfect for reheating a few muffins.

PARTY
MUFFINS

LEMON POPPY SEED MUFFINS

These moist, fluffy seed cakes are bursting with delicate flavors. The secret to keeping the seeds moist is first cooking them with honey.

½ cup poppy seeds
2 tablespoons honey
2 tablespoons water
3 tablespoons lemon juice
1 stick butter, softened
½ cup sugar
2 eggs
1 tablespoon grated lemon zest
¾ cup plain yogurt
1¾ cups all-purpose flour
1 teaspoon baking soda
2 teaspoons baking powder
½ teaspoon salt

Combine poppy seeds, honey, and water in small saucepan and place over medium heat. Cook, stirring frequently, until seeds are evenly moistened and mixture resembles wet sand, about 4 minutes. Let cool and then stir in lemon juice.

Preheat oven to 375 degrees F. Grease muffin tins or line with paper cups.

In large mixing bowl, cream butter and sugar until smooth. Beat in eggs, zest, and yogurt. Mix in seed mixture.

In another bowl, combine flour, baking soda, powder and salt. Add dry ingredients to liquid and stir until combined. Fill muffin cups to top. Bake about 20 minutes, until tops are golden and center is done when tested.

MAKES 12

CANDIED GINGER LEMON MUFFINS

These sunny yellow muffins are just what the doctor ordered for a rainy day in bed or for teatime.

1 cup cake flour
1 cup all-purpose flour
1 ½ teaspoons baking soda
6 tablespoons butter, softened
¾ cup sugar
2 teaspoons grated lemon zest
2 eggs
1 cup half-and-half
3 tablespoons lemon juice
½ cup crystallized ginger, rinsed, dried and chopped
12 thin slices lemon, optional

Preheat oven to 375 degrees F. Grease muffin tins or line with paper cups.

Combine two flours and baking soda in bowl. Mix with fork.

In another bowl, cream together butter and sugar. Beat in lemon zest. Add eggs one at a time, beating after each addition. Pour in half-and-half and lemon juice and mix until combined. Add flour mixture. Stir just until flour disappears. Gently stir in chopped ginger.

Spoon into muffin cups and top each with lemon slice, if desired. Bake about 20 minutes, until tester comes out clean.

MAKES 12

DEEP CHOCOLATE SOUR CHERRY MUFFINS

These are so rich and chocolatey you can get away with serving them as cupcakes for a children's party. Dust the tops with confectioners' sugar for special occasions.

¾ cup dried sour cherries
¼ cup kirsch
1 stick butter
6 ounces bittersweet chocolate, chopped
3 eggs
½ cup sugar
⅔ cup sour cream
1¾ cups all-purpose flour
2 teaspoons baking powder
½ teaspoon baking soda

Preheat oven to 375 degrees F. Grease muffin tins or line with paper cups.

Combine dried cherries and kirsch in small saucepan. Cook over low heat until liquid is absorbed. Set aside to cool.

In medium heavy saucepan, combine butter and chocolate. Cook over low heat, stirring constantly, until both are melted and smooth. Set aside to cool.

With electric mixer, beat eggs with sugar until light and fluffy. Beat in sour cream. Then pour in chocolate mixture and stir to combine.

In another bowl, stir together flour, baking powder and soda. Add to the chocolate mixture and mix just until flour disappears. Gently stir in cherries and fill muffin cups to top. Bake 20 to 25 minutes, until tester comes out clean.

MAKES 12

PECAN CINNAMON MUFFINS

These rich, miniature coffee cakes are perfect for quick company breakfasts and afternoon espresso.

1 cup pecan halves
1 ¼ teaspoons cinnamon
1 tablespoon brown sugar
1 stick butter, softened
1 cup sugar
2 eggs
1 cup sour cream
1 tablespoon vanilla
2 cups all-purpose flour
1 tablespoon baking powder
¼ teaspoon salt

Preheat oven to 350 degrees F. Grease muffin tin or line with paper cups. Toast pecans on baking tray in oven about 10 minutes. Roughly chop three-quarters of the nuts into large chunks and reserve. Finely chop remaining pecans. Mix in small bowl with $\frac{1}{4}$ teaspoon cinnamon and brown sugar. Set aside for topping.

Cream together butter and sugar until light and fluffy. Beat in eggs, sour cream and vanilla.

In another bowl combine flour, baking powder, salt, and remaining teaspoon cinnamon. Add flour mixture to liquid and stir just until flour disappears. Lightly stir in chopped pecans.

Fill muffin cups to the top. Sprinkle each with generous teaspoon brown sugar topping. Bake about 25 minutes, until tester comes out clean. Let cool 5 minutes, then lift out from tops and edges to avoid spilling.

MAKES 12

ORANGE MARMALADE MUFFINS

A triple orange treat: zest, orange liqueur and orange marmalade. For a variation, omit the marmalade and stir two-third's cup mini chocolate chips into the batter.

¾ stick butter, softened
¾ cup sugar
2 eggs
1 tablespoon grated orange zest
¾ cup heavy cream
2 tablespoons Grand Marnier or other
    orange liqueur
2 cups all-purpose flour
1 tablespoon baking powder
¼ teaspoon salt
¼ cup orange marmalade

Preheat oven to 400 degrees F. Grease muffin tins or line with paper cups.

With electric mixer, cream butter and sugar until smooth. Add eggs, one at a time, beating well after each. Add orange zest, cream, and Grand Marnier. Beat to combine.

In another bowl, stir together flour, baking powder and salt. Add to liquid ingredients and gently beat until flour just disappears.

Spoon 1 generous tablespoon batter into each of 10 muffin cups and smooth to cover bottom. Place 1 teaspoon orange marmalade in the center, then top with another tablespoonful of batter to cover. Bake 20 minutes, until tops are golden and slightly cracked.

MAKES 10

PEANUT BUTTER CHOCOLATE CHIP MUFFINS

A guaranteed hit at your next preschool potluck or childish occasion! For peanut butter and jelly purists, place a pocket of strawberry jam or preserves in the center (see previous recipe) and omit the chips.

1 cup chunky peanut butter, softened
1 egg
$\frac{1}{3}$ cup brown sugar
$\frac{1}{3}$ cup sugar
1 cup milk
1$\frac{1}{2}$ cups whole wheat flour
1 tablespoon baking powder
$\frac{1}{2}$ cup mini chocolate chips

Preheat oven to 375 degrees F. Grease muffin tins or line with paper cups.

With electric mixer, beat peanut butter, egg, and sugars until smooth. Add milk in 3 parts, mixing between additions to blend. Add flour and baking powder and mix just until flour disappears. Beat in chocolate chips. Spoon into muffin cups and bake about 20 minutes, until tester comes out clean.

MAKES 12

WHITEOUT MUFFINS

For vanilla lovers, a great big white-on-white hunk of cake disguised as a muffin.

       1 stick butter, softened
       3/4 cup sugar
       2 eggs
       1 tablespoon vanilla
       1 cup half-and-half
       1 1/2 cups all-purpose flour
       1/2 cup + 2 tablespoons cake flour
       1 tablespoon baking powder
       1/4 teaspoon salt
       1/2 cup macadamia nuts, toasted and
          chopped
       3/4 cup vanilla or white chocolate chips

Preheat oven to 350 degrees F. Grease muffin tins or line with paper cups.

Cream the butter until fluffy. Slowly add sugar, continuing to beat. Add eggs, one at a time, beating after each. Add vanilla and half-and-half. Beat until evenly blended.

In another bowl, mix together two flours, baking powder, and salt. Add to liquid mixture and beat just until flour disappears. Gently stir in nuts and chips. Fill muffin cups to the top, and bake 30 to 35 minutes until slightly golden on the edges and a tester comes out clean.

MAKES 12

SWEET POTATO MUFFINS

*A timeless contribution to Thanksgiving dinner from
Julie Simon.*

1 stick butter, softened
1 cup sugar
1 ¼ cup canned, pureed sweet potatoes
   or yams
2 eggs
1 ¼ cups milk
1 teaspoon lemon extract
2 ½ cups all-purpose flour
1 ½ tablespoons baking powder
¾ teaspoon nutmeg
½ teaspoon salt
1 teaspoon cinnamon
½ cup chopped, toasted pecans
¼ cup sugar mixed with 1 tablespoon
   cinnamon for topping

Preheat oven to 400 degrees F. Grease two muffin tins or line with paper cups.

Cream butter and sugar until light and fluffy. Beat in sweet potatoes or yams. Beat in eggs, one at a time. Beat in milk and lemon extract.

In another bowl, combine flour, baking powder, nutmeg, salt and cinnamon. Add to liquid mixture and mix just until flour disappears. Stir in nuts. Spoon batter into muffin cups, sprinkle tops with cinnamon sugar and bake 20 to 25 minutes until a tester comes out clean.

MAKES 24

RASPBERRY CHEESECAKE MUFFINS

A pretty addition to the morning bread basket.

> 1 (3-ounce) package cream cheese, room temperature
> 3 eggs
> 1 cup sugar
> 1½ teaspoons vanilla
> 6 tablespoons butter
> 2 cups all-purpose flour
> 1 cup milk
> 2½ teaspoons baking powder
> ½ teaspoon salt
> 1 cup raspberries, fresh or frozen, (unthawed)

Preheat oven to 400 degrees F. Grease Muffin tins or line with paper cups.

In small bowl, beat cream cheese with 1 egg, ¼ cup sugar, and ½ teaspoon vanilla until smooth. Set aside.

In saucepan, combine milk, butter, and remaining teaspoon vanilla. Stir over medium heat until butter melts. Cool until warm to touch, then beat in remaining 2 eggs.

In large bowl, combine flour, baking powder, salt, and remaining ¾ cup sugar. Add milk mixture and stir just to blend. Fold in raspberries. Divide batter equally among muffin cups. Spoon about 2 teaspoons cream cheese mixture on top of each muffin. Pull knife through each top to swirl slightly. Bake about 20 minutes or until tops spring back when lightly touched.

MAKES 12

GRAHAM CRACKER MUFFINS

These were a happy accident that occurred when
found a box of graham cracker crumbs in the
They are excellent for a child's party or lunch

2½ cups graham cracker crum
½ cup all-purpose flour
½ cup sugar
2½ teaspoons baking powder
1 cup milk
1 egg, lightly beaten
1 cup milk chocolate chips
½ cup coarsely chopped peanuts

Preheat oven to 400 degrees F. Grease
muffin tins or line with paper cups.

In bowl, combine crumbs, flour, sugar, and baking powder.

Add milk and egg and stir just until moistened. Fold in chocolate and nuts. Divide batter among muffin cups.

Bake 15 to 20 minutes or until tops spring back when lightly pressed.

MAKES 12

PEACH COBBLER MUFFINS

These individual cobblers are terrific for a summer picnic.

1½ cups all-purpose flour
½ cup plus 4 teaspoons sugar
2½ teaspoons baking powder
¼ teaspoon salt
6 tablespoons butter, chilled and diced
1 cup milk
1½ cups coarsely chopped, peeled
    peaches, fresh or frozen
1½ tablespoons butter, melted
½ teaspoon cinnamon

Preheat oven to 400 degrees F. Grease muffin tins or line with paper cups.

In bowl, combine flour, ½ cup sugar, baking powder, and salt. Using pastry blender or two knives, cut in diced butter until crumbly. Stir in milk. Add peaches and stir to distribute evenly. Divide dough evenly among prepared cups.

Drizzle tops with melted butter. Combine remaining 4 teaspoons sugar and cinnamon and sprinkle over muffins. Bake 25 minutes or until muffins are golden.

MAKES 9

TROPICAL UPSIDE-DOWN MUFFINS

These rich cakes are great desserts for summer barbecues.

1½ sticks butter
¾ cup brown sugar
¾ cup chopped fresh pineapple
¾ cup chopped papaya
¾ cup papaya nectar
2 eggs, lightly beaten
1¾ cups all-purpose flour
¾ cup sugar
2 teaspoons baking powder
¼ teaspoon salt
¾ cup chopped macadamia nuts

Preheat oven to 350 degrees F. Grease 12 (4-ounce) custard cups or ramekins.

Melt ½ stick butter. Stir in brown sugar, pineapple, and papaya. Stir over medium heat until sugar is melted. Divide mixture evenly among prepared cups.

In pan, combine remaining stick butter and papaya nectar. Heat, stirring, just until butter melts. Cool to lukewarm, then stir in eggs.

In bowl, combine flour, sugar, baking powder and salt.

Stir in liquid mixture just until dry ingredients are moistened. Stir in nuts. Spoon batter over fruit in cups.

Arrange on baking sheet and bake 25 minutes or until muffins spring back when lightly pressed.

To serve, run thin knife around edges of each muffin to loosen. Invert onto serving plates. Serve warm.

MAKES 12

CARAMEL APPLE MUFFINS

If your idea of heaven is a place where caramel apples are served for breakfast, here is the muffin for you.

2 cups all-purpose flour
¾ cup sugar
2¼ teaspoons cinnamon
½ teaspoon salt
1 egg, lightly beaten
1 cup milk
½ stick butter, melted
1½ teaspoons vanilla
½ cup peeled, finely diced apple
¾ cup diced caramel candy squares
(about 12)

Preheat oven to 350 degrees F. Grease muffin tins or line with paper cups.

In large bowl, combine flour, sugar, baking powder, cinnamon, and salt.

In another bowl, combine egg and milk. Stir in butter and vanilla. Add flour mixture and stir just to blend. Stir in apples and caramels. Divide batter among prepared cups. Bake 25 minutes or until tops spring back when lightly pressed. Serve warm.

MAKES 12

RHUBARB CUSTARD MUFFINS

A pocketful of rich custard nicely offsets the tartness of rhubarb in this cozy muffin.

2 egg yolks
4 teaspoons sugar
2½ teaspoons vanilla
½ cup hot milk
¾ cup brown sugar
⅓ cup vegetable oil
1 egg
1 cup buttermilk
1½ cups diced fresh or frozen rhubarb
2½ cups all-purpose flour
1½ teaspoons baking powder
1½ teaspoons baking soda
½ teaspoon salt

In heavy saucepan, whisk yolks and granulated sugar until light. Whisk in hot milk. Cook over medium heat, stirring constantly, until thick, about 6 minutes. Stir in $\frac{1}{2}$ teaspoon vanilla. Chill.

Preheat oven to 350 degrees F. Line muffin tin with paper cups.

In large bowl, combine brown sugar, oil, egg, buttermilk, and remaining 2 teaspoons vanilla. Beat to blend. Stir in rhubarb.

In another bowl, combine flour, baking powder, soda, and salt. Add to rhubarb mixture and stir just until moistened.

Divide batter evenly among muffin cups. Using measuring tablespoon, press in center of each to form a pool. Fill each with scant tablespoon of chilled custard.

Bake 20 minutes or until golden brown.

MAKES 12

SAVORY
MUFFINS

FIG ANISEED MUFFINS

Our idea of waking up in heaven—fig jam on a fig muffin. No butter needed.

1 egg
1 cup milk
¼ cup vegetable oil
2 teaspoons anise extract
1¼ cups all-purpose flour
½ cup whole wheat flour
1 tablespoon baking powder
½ teaspoon salt
2 tablespoons sugar
1 tablespoon aniseeds
½ cup chopped, dried figs

Preheat oven to 375 degrees F. Grease muffin tins or line with paper cups.

In large mixing bowl, whisk together egg, milk, oil, and anise extract.

In another bowl, combine flour, whole wheat flour, baking powder, salt, sugar, and aniseeds. Stir with fork. Add dry ingredients to liquid. Stir until evenly moistened. Stir in figs and spoon into muffin cups. Bake 15 to 20 minutes or until tester comes out clean.

MAKES 10

Cooling Your Muffins

The best test for doneness is to insert a toothpick in the center of the largest muffin. If it comes out clean, without wet particles clinging to it, the batch is done. Let muffins sit in the trays about 5 minutes to set and then invert onto a rack, turn right-side-up and let cool about 10 minutes before serving. Cool completely before freezing.

CHILE CORN MUFFINS

The chile flavor in these moist, flavor-filled muffins develops over time.

1 cup all-purpose flour
1 cup cornmeal
1 tablespoon baking powder
1 teaspoon cumin
¾ teaspoon salt
¼ teaspoon red chile flakes
1 egg
½ cup sour cream
¾ cup milk
½ stick butter, melted
½ cup grated cheddar cheese
1 jalapeño chile pepper, seeded
    and diced
¾ cup drained canned corn

Preheat oven to 350 degrees F. Grease muffin tins or line with paper cups.

In large mixing bowl, combine flour, cornmeal, baking powder, cumin, salt, and red chile flakes. Stir and set aside.

In another bowl, whisk egg. Stir in sour cream, milk, melted butter, cheese, jalapeño, and corn. Add dry ingredients and stir to combine. Fill muffin cups to top and bake 30 to 35 minutes, until tester comes out clean.

MAKES 12

TOASTED WALNUT GORGONZOLA MUFFINS

This classic combination is delicious served warm, while the cheese is still runny, with sliced fresh pears.

1 egg
½ stick butter, melted and cooled
1 cup low fat milk
½ cup crumbled gorgonzola or blue cheese
1½ cups all-purpose flour
2½ teaspoons baking powder
¼ teaspoon salt
¾ cup toasted walnuts, chopped

Preheat oven to 375 degrees F. Grease muffin tins or line with paper cups.

Whisk egg in large mixing bowl. Add butter, milk and cheese. Whisk to combine and set aside.

In another bowl, combine flour, baking powder and salt. Mix with fork. Add to liquid ingredients and stir to combine. Stir in walnuts and spoon into muffin cups. Bake about 20 minutes until slightly brown and cheese begins to bubble. Serve warm.

MAKES 12

Nutty Muffins

We love the crunch and flavor of nuts in our muffins. For impromptu muffin baking keep a selection of nuts in the freezer. They do not need to be defrosted but all nuts do benefit from a slight toasting to develop flavor. Just spread on a tray and bake in a 350 F oven 10 to 15 minutes, shaking the pan occasionally. Let cool and then chop.

ROSEMARY MUFFINS

These tender, light muffins would be a refreshing choice for afternoon tea.

1 cup milk
2 tablespoons fresh rosemary, chopped
2 teaspoons lemon zest, grated
2 cups all-purpose flour
1½ teaspoons baking powder
½ teaspoon salt
2 eggs
1 stick butter, melted
2 tablespoons sugar

Preheat oven to 375 degrees F. Grease muffin tins or line with paper cups.

In small pan, combine milk, rosemary and lemon zest. Bring to simmer and cook over low heat 2 minutes. Cool.

In bowl, combine flour, baking powder, and salt.

In large bowl beat eggs until frothy. Beat in butter, sugar, and then cooled milk mixture. Stir in dry ingredients just until moistened. Spoon batter equally among 9 muffin cups. Bake about 20 minutes or until tester comes out clean.

MAKES 9

The Zest

Zest, or the outer, colored layer of skin on citrus fruit, adds a much more intense shot of flavor to baked goods than juice alone. The easiest way to remove it, is by rubbing against the smallest side of a grater and then chopping. Always wash and dry the lemon or orange first and then store zested fruit in the refrigerator for another use. (If a recipe calls for both zest and juice, remove zest first.) Do not remove zest far in advance, since the delicate oils dry quickly and the flavor will fade.

SUN-DRIED TOMATO OLIVE MUFFINS

These red- and black-flecked muffins are a good choice to serve with egg and cheese dishes.

> 2 cups all-purpose flour
> 1 tablespoon baking powder
> ½ teaspoon salt
> 1 egg
> 3 tablespoons oil drained from tomatoes
> 2 tablespoons sugar
> 1 cup milk
> ¼ cup chopped, drained oil-packed sun-dried tomatoes
> ½ cup chopped, pitted Kalamata olives

Preheat oven to 375 degrees F. Grease muffin tins or line with paper cups.

In large bowl, combine flour, baking powder, and salt.

In another bowl, lightly beat egg. Stir in tomato oil, sugar and milk. Pour all at once into flour mixture. Mix just until flour disappears. Stir in chopped tomatoes and olives. Divide among muffin cups. Bake 25 minutes, or until muffins spring back when pressed.

MAKES 9

POTATO CHIVE MUFFINS

Serve these moist, peppery muffins with a casual soup or salad supper.

> 3 cups grated, peeled, boiling potatoes, uncooked
> 1/4 cup chopped fresh chives
> 3 eggs
> 1 stick butter, melted
> 1 cup all-purpose flour
> 1 teaspoon baking powder
> 1 teaspoon salt
> 1/2 teaspoon freshly ground black pepper

Preheat oven to 400 degrees F. Grease muffin tins or line with paper cups.

In bowl, whisk together potatoes, chives, eggs, and butter.

In another bowl, combine flour, baking powder, salt, and pepper. Add to potato mixture and stir to blend. Spoon batter into muffin cups and bake 20 minutes or until a tester comes out clean.

MAKES 12

ONION CARAWAY MUFFINS

The flavors of rye bread baked into an easy muffin.

2 tablespoons butter
1/2 cup diced onion
1 1/2 tablespoons caraway seeds
1 3/4 cups all-purpose flour
2 teaspoons baking powder
1 teaspoon baking soda
1/2 teaspoon salt
2 eggs
1 cup sour cream
1/4 cup vegetable oil
1/2 cup milk

Preheat oven to 350 degrees F. Grease muffin tins or line with paper cups.

Melt butter in small skillet over medium heat. Saute onions with caraway seeds until soft and slightly brown. Set aside.

Combine flour, baking powder, soda, and salt in mixing bowl.

In another bowl, whisk eggs until smooth. Stir in sour cream, oil, milk, and onion mixture. Pour into flour mixture and mix until evenly moistened. Spoon into muffin cups and bake 15 to 20 minutes, until a tester comes out clean.

MAKES 12

PARMESAN HERB MUFFINS

A nice and cheesy choice for a soup or salad supper.

1 egg
¼ cup olive oil
1 cup low-fat milk
1 cup grated Parmesan cheese
2 tablespoons fresh basil, oregano,
    or tarragon, chopped
1 cup all-purpose flour
⅓ cup cornmeal
2½ teaspoons baking powder

Preheat oven to 375 degrees F. Grease muffin tins or line with paper cups.

In large mixing bowl, whisk together egg, olive oil, milk, Parmesan, and fresh herbs. Set aside.

In another bowl, combine flour, cornmeal, and baking powder. Mix with fork and then add to liquid ingredients. Stir just to combine and spoon batter into muffin cups. Bake 15 to 20 minutes, until a tester comes out clean.

MAKES 10